DATE DUE		
DE 02 '03		
FE 02 '05		
DE 18 '06		
DE 03 '07		
APR 2 2 '08		
DEC 2 2 '10		
FEB 0 7 '11		
MAR 1 5 '11		

20TH CENTURY MEDIA

1990s

ELECTRONIC MEDIA

Please visit our web site at: www.garethstevens.com
For a free color catalog describing Gareth Stevens Publishing's
list of high-quality books and multimedia programs, call
1-800-542-2595 (USA) or 1-800-387-3178 (Canada).
Gareth Stevens Publishing's fax: (414) 332-3567.

Library of Congress Cataloging-in-Publication Data

Parker, Steve.
    20th century media / by Steve Parker.
       v. cm.
    Includes bibliographical references and index.
    Contents: [1] 1900–20: print to pictures. [2] 20s & 30s: entertainment for all.
[3] 40s & 50s: power and persuasion. [4] 1960s: the Satellite Age. [5] 70s & 80s:
global technology. [6] 1990s: electronic media.
    ISBN 0-8368-3182-9 (v. 1: lib. bdg.) — ISBN 0-8368-3183-7 (v. 2: lib. bdg.) —
ISBN 0-8368-3184-5 (v. 3: lib. bdg.) — ISBN 0-8368-3185-3 (v. 4: lib. bdg.) —
ISBN 0-8368-3186-1 (v. 5: lib. bdg.) — ISBN 0-8368-3187-X (v. 6: lib. bdg.)
    1. Mass media—History—20th century—Juvenile literature. [1. Mass
media—History—20th century.] I. Title: Twentieth century media. II. Title.
P91.2.P37   2002
302.23'09'04—dc21   2002022556

This North American edition first published in 2002 by
Gareth Stevens Publishing
A World Almanac Education Group Company
330 West Olive Street, Suite 100
Milwaukee, Wisconsin 53212 USA

Original edition © 2002 by David West Children's Books. First published in Great Britain
in 2002 by Heinemann Library, Halley Court, Jordan Hill, Oxford OX2 8EJ, a division of Reed
Educational and Professional Publishing Limited. This U.S. edition © 2002 by Gareth Stevens, Inc.
Additional end matter © 2002 by Gareth Stevens, Inc.

Designer: Rob Shone
Editor: James Pickering
Picture Research: Carrie Haines

Gareth Stevens Editor: Dorothy L. Gibbs

Photo Credits:
Abbreviations: (t) top, (m) middle, (b) bottom, (l) left, (r) right

Dave Benett @ Alpha London: page 25(tl).
BSkyB: pages 5(bl), 8(br), 17(tl), 26(bl), 27(mr).
Castrol: pages 26-27(background), 27(t).
Corbis Stock Market: pages 3, 5(mr), 8(tl).
Courtesy of Apple Macintosh: pages 4-5, 9(tl).
The Defence Picture Library: page 15(br).
The Kobal Collection: pages 5(t), 20(tl), 20-21, 21(br, bl), 22(br), 22-23, 23(tr).
NASA: cover (bl).
Popperfoto: pages 26-27(b); Reuters: cover (m), pages 4(b), 6, 7(tr, m), 9(tr, br), 11(ml), 12(t), 13(tl),
    14-15(m, t), 15(tr), 16(both), 17(r, bm), 18(tr), 19(mr), 20(b), 23(bl, br), 24-25, 25(b), 28(all).
Redferns/Giovanni De Bei: page 24(tl); Kieran Doherty: page 25(mr).
Rex Features: pages 7(bl, br), 10(bl).
Topham Picturepoint: page 18(b); Press Association: page 29(tr).

Printed in the United States of America

1 2 3 4 5 6 7 8 9 06 05 04 03 02

20TH CENTURY MEDIA

1990_S

ELECTRONIC MEDIA

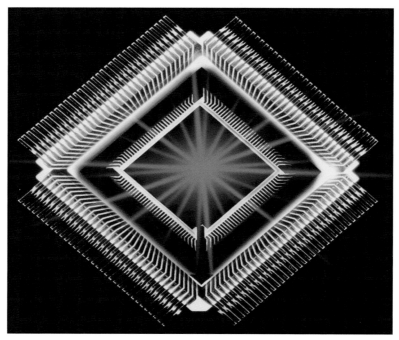

Steve Parker

Gareth Stevens Publishing
A WORLD ALMANAC EDUCATION GROUP COMPANY

CONTENTS

A mouse is like the handle of a door (the computer) to a different universe — the Internet. During the 1990s, computers became faster and more powerful than ever. They even took over some of the roles previously filled by TV, videotapes, and music recordings.

The Internet can help anyone with a computer and a phone link find out anything, anywhere. For journalists, it is an ideal medium to get news stories to a global public in seconds. But will future generations be lost to cyberspace?

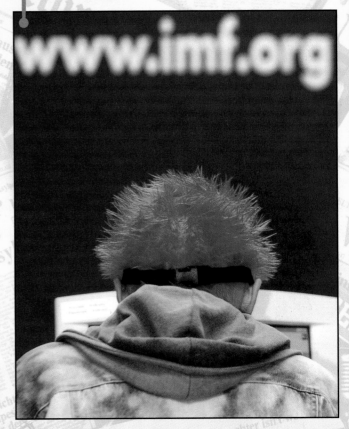

NEWEST AND BIGGEST

Television, Page 9

Near the end of the 20th century, the film world produced a tidal wave of special effects, but they were no guarantee of success.

Although digital TV has brought us hundreds of new 24-hour channels, people still complain that there's nothing on.

Media experts made an amazing calculation at the end of the 20th century. More words and pictures had been made available to the public in the last four years of the century than in all the rest of the century — and in all of the centuries before! At the start of the 20th century, the main media for information and entertainment were printed newspapers and books and some visual media, such as art and theater. Then came radio, movies, recorded sound, television, satellite and cable, video, CDs, DVDs, and many other new formats. The record-breaking output in the 20th century's last four years, however, was due to the phenomenal growth and power of the Internet. Where will this amazing new medium take us in the 21st century?

During the 1990s, more telecommunication towers to support more mobile phones and other wireless technology led to a new medium — the text message.

5

FREEDOM FOR ALL

To some, he was a freedom fighter. To others, he was a terrorist. Nelson Mandela was imprisoned for twenty-seven years for the crime of trying to overthrow the South African government by sabotage. No pictures of him were allowed during these years. Then, in 1990, he appeared on global television — a free man. Four years later, he was president of his newly united nation.

The release of Nelson Mandela, shown here with his wife, Winnie, generated intense excitement, partly to see what he looked like after twenty-seven years. The 1960s South African government had regarded Mandela's acts as terrorism, but to people who believed in freedom for all, his actions were for a just cause.

DISRUPTING APARTHEID

Nelson Mandela (*b.* 1918) grew up in the Transkei region of South Africa and studied law in Johannesburg. In 1944, he joined the African National Congress (ANC), a group dedicated to gaining equal rights for all people in South Africa. At the time, a racist system known as apartheid gave only white South Africans full rights. In 1962, Mandela was jailed for his part in disruptive campaigns to destroy targets, such as electricity towers.

RELEASE DAY

As the anti-apartheid struggle continued, it involved many kinds of media, from reports in newspapers and on TV and radio to powerful works of music, poetry, drama, and visual arts. Finally, South Africa's white-elected government, led by F. W. de Klerk, recognized a need for change. On February 11, 1990, Mandela walked out of Victor Verster Prison, near Cape Town, into a media frenzy. It was the first time he had been seen in public since 1962.

Working as a lawyer during the 1950s, Mandela tried to defeat apartheid by peaceful means.

Mandela and de Klerk, both lawyers, had great respect for each other. De Klerk became South Africa's second deputy president.

A NEW ERA

Mandela had lost none of his desire to gain justice and freedom for all citizens. In 1994, South Africa held its first election in which any adult, regardless of color, could vote. The ANC triumphed, and Mandela became president. The world's media and its public were spellbound with awe and respect, and Mandela's became the best-known face on the planet.

In May 1994, the news media covered the South African elections in great detail.

CELEBRATION

Many musicians, singers, and recording artists campaigned against South African apartheid. In 1990, a huge concert was held at London's Wembley Stadium to celebrate Nelson Mandela's release. When Mandela appeared as special guest, the crowd went wild.

The International Tribute for a Free South Africa concert, April 16, 1990

7

DIGITAL FUTURE

Digits are numbers, such as 1, 2, and 3. Digital systems are based on numbers. Information in digital systems, including words, pictures, and sounds, is represented as codes of numbers. Why are digital systems important, and how have they affected media?

Infrastructures for mobile phones sprang up like giant weeds in the 1990s.

The year 2000 mobile phone was one-tenth the size of the 1990 version. G3 (third generation) mobiles offered Internet access by means of an on-screen display.

DIGITAL VERSUS ANALOG

Computers are digital, with a binary system of two digits: 1 (a short pulse of electricity) and 0 (no pulse). All information, data, instructions, and programs in a computer are in the form of binary digits, or "bits" — billions of them! CDs and DVDs are also digital. Radio and television, however, which started before digital technology was advanced, were analog, with signals coded in the form of continuously varying up and down waves. Audio and video cassettes and most telephones were analog, too.

BY THE NUMBERS

During the 1990s, radio and TV began the switch to digital. Instead of waves, their signals went out as ultrafast streams of on-off digital pulses. Three to ten times as many TV or radio channels can be squeezed into the batch of signals used for just one analog channel. Digital is higher quality, too, with clearer sounds and sharper pictures. Because digital is less prone to error than analog, information is transferred almost perfectly from one form to another as it passes through the broadcasting system.

To delay buying a new digital TV set, a decoder box can receive TV broadcasts in digital form and convert them into analog signals for a traditional TV set.

The screen of a normal TV is a heavy, bulky, glass "tube." Liquid-crystal technology, a 1990s' advancement, gave streamlined flat screens the same picture quality as tubes.

ANOTHER FAD?

Digital data, such as sounds and pictures, can be stored on CDs and DVDs and fed directly into a computer to be manipulated. By 2000, digital TV and radio had made an impact, yet people worried that expensive digital equipment might be just a fad and would quickly be overtaken by further advancements. Many decided to wait and see, some running digital and analog media side by side.

In 1998, Apple computers started a new design trend with the colorful and curvy Internet Macintosh, or iMac. This easy-to-use computer was marketed less as a work tool and more as a fashion accessory and even as a friendly personal "pet."

SHRINKING WORLD

Smaller "chips" and other devices enabled electronic media equipment, such as computers, telephones, and radios, to shrink through the decade. Desktop became laptop. Then, laptop became palmtop, so you could hold it in your hand. Personal digital assistants, or PDAs, are electronic diaries or notebooks. They allow basic computing functions on the move, to feed into a main computer back home or at the office.

A 1997 digital car radio

Too much TV?

Analog, digital, ground-based, satellite, cable, new programs, endless reruns, dozens of stations, hundreds of channels, local and national, 24-hour broadcasting, on-demand movies, videos and DVDs, interactivity — the world's number one medium has it all. Can people still complain "there's nothing on TV?"

MORE CHOICE

The digital revolution meant more TV channels and programs than ever before. Some of TV's "extra capacity," its ability to carry more and more information, was used to offer wider consumer choice. For a program such as a sports event, for example, a viewer could choose which camera angles to see, which slow-motion replays to watch, and the language for the commentary. In the United Kingdom, the BSkyB satellite company took away many major sports events from the BBC and ITV networks, then charged people to view them. Pay-TV was expected to spread in the new millennium.

Which king was married to Eleanor of Aquitaine?

- A: Henry I
- B: Henry II
- C: Richard I
- D: Henry V

Quiz shows, which had been very popular in the 1950s, came back in the 1990s with huge cash prizes. Each show had special features, such as "lifelines" on Who Wants to Be a Millionaire?

LESS CHOICE

The glut of TV channels and programs did not extend around the world. The most populated nation, China, had only one major network, China Central Television (CCTV). It ran about ten channels, some of them broadcasting only a few hours a day, and all of them under the strict control of communist state authorities.

10

More channels and shows for children were added through the 1990s. Would too much TV make children pale and weak? This debate dates back fifty years.

TELEVISIONS EVERYWHERE

Putting televisions in public places has been a topic of debate since the medium entered daily life in the late 1940s. A growing alliance between television and sports led to the idea of sports bars with big TV screens showing live and recorded sports from around the world. Massive replay screens at live events were another development.

The local sports bar offers a social setting for watching televised sports events.

For the reality game show Big Brother, contestants were isolated from the outside world for up to nine weeks. TV cameras spied on them 24 hours a day, and barbed wire kept out unwelcome visitors.

INTERACTIVE TV

A new role for TV in the early 1990s was interactive, or two-way, transmission. Interactive TV was expected to grow enormously. In 1996, however, Time Warner's Full Service Network (FSN), the first interactive cable channel in the United States, did not pass its two-year trial period. With the expansion of the Internet, computer interaction grew faster than the TV version.

By means of a phone link, interactive TV lets viewers feed in, as well as get out, information through a TV set. On a shopping channel, they can flick through the screens to order items on the spot.

THE "NET" SPREADS

The Internet has grown bigger and faster than any other medium in history. Businesses, schools, governments, organizations, and even private individuals have Web sites that make their information available to the world.

Almost every office has computers, not only for accounting and for storing employee information, but also to communicate. A company's computers may be linked, by wires and a device called a server, into a network.

12

WWW.WOW!

The Internet is a global system of computers joined by the wires and cables, as well as the microwave, satellite, and radio links, of telecommunication networks. Parts of the Net are private, such as electronic mail, or e-mail, messages people send to each other or the information companies send between their offices. The World Wide Web (WWW) is a part of the Internet that anyone can access using a computer and a telephone line. The Web is truly multimedia — a giant electronic library of words, pictures, sounds, games, animation, and much more.

NETS AND WEBS

The Internet uses the same routes as telephones, the telecommunication networks of metal wires, fiber-optic cables, microwave towers, and satellite links. Each region has an access point called a gateway, which is like a huge computer, the Internet equivalent of a major telephone exchange. A gateway directs information and messages to subnets, which serve smaller areas and route information to its final destination.

UNBELIEVABLE GROWTH

In about 1993, the World Wide Web had less than a hundred named sites. By January 1996, the number was 100,000; by April 1997, over a million. Early in 2000, the number of sites rocketed past 10 million. By the end of that year, the number reached a staggering 25 million, offering everything from sports and music to the history of origami, the Japanese art of paper folding, and giant shopping malls.

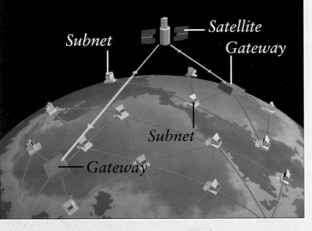

Subnet
Satellite
Gateway
Subnet
Gateway

Rowntree (left) and Lamacq at Café Cyberia

CYBER CAFÉS

Just as TV screens appeared in sports bars, computer screens linked to the Internet showed up in cafés. Cyber cafés offer refreshment, relaxation, and on-line information, or simply virtual fun, either alone or with friends. Steve Lamacq, a popular BBC Radio One disk jockey, and Dave Rowntree, a drummer with the British rock band Blur, hosted Europe's first live radio show from a cyber café. Listeners sent in music during the show — via the Internet.

CYBERSPACE

The Internet is an unreal or virtual world called "cyberspace." It is an electronic place that exists only as tiny electrical pulses in computer circuits. Cyberspace presents endlessly flexible multimedia for use by advertisers, shoppers, businesses, public services such as libraries, special interest groups such as bottle-top collectors, and anyone else.

Sites on the World Wide Web range from companies trying to attract more business to individuals just having a good time.

13

E-mail is similar to letters sent through the postal service. Messages go privately, direct from sender to receiver, but they arrive in seconds, rather than days.

MEDIA INVASION

By the 1990s, tiny microphones, cameras, radio transmitters, and other gadgets could turn anyone into James Bond. Spying on people and their secrets was easy, but was it legal? Even if it was, should it be done at all?

RIGHT TO PRIVACY

Hidden "bug" microphones, remote-control cameras, and phone or computer "taps" are the modern equivalents of peeking through a keyhole. Like private detectives and spies, media photographers and reporters sometimes use undercover methods that are legally doubtful. If they expose serious crime or corruption, most people agree the methods are justified. But what if they invade a person's private life and cause the person severe grief just to sell more newspapers or to boost TV ratings?

SPY IN THE SKY

Battery pack

Rotors powered by a quiet electric motor

Small stills or video camera

Radio control receiver

Microphone

A radio-controlled model helicopter with an onboard camera is a sneaky spy for taking photos. In case the craft is captured or damaged, pictures are sent by radio to a receiver as they are taken. This kind of camera has many worthwhile uses, such as surveying dangerous crash scenes. Its use by the media is much more controversial.

Almost every day, Princess Diana was subjected to intense media scrutiny. Photographers swarmed around her to take pictures. Ordinary life is impossible under such relentlessly stressful conditions.

14

The paparazzi are photographers who will use almost any trick to get unusual or desirable pictures to sell to the highest bidders. Although people often throw up their hands in horror at paparazzi methods, they buy the pictures, thereby creating the need for them.

THE MOST FAMOUS FACE

The world's most photographed person of the 1990s was probably Diana, Princess of Wales. She married the heir to the British throne, Prince Charles, in 1981, but personal problems led to their separation. Diana was beautiful, fashionable, and kindhearted, and she worked tirelessly for the disadvantaged and the poor. She was also vulnerable and often unhappy. Her life was a fascinating mixture of success and tragedy, and her face on a magazine or a newspaper was bound to increase its sales.

SUDDEN LOSS

In 1997, Diana's death in a car crash stunned the world. Accusations flew that the media were to blame. Had reporters and photographers, who were always following Diana's every move, caused the crash? Although the media were judged to be innocent, the event served to highlight the dangers of excessive media attention.

LOOKING FOR BLAME

After Diana's death, people asked who was to blame. Eager, as always, to satisfy public demand, the media pounced on some of its own workers, especially the paparazzi. Roles were reversed as photographers suddenly felt the glare of the media spotlight and had to prove their innocence in contributing to the fatal crash.

Photographers had to publicly justify their involvement in the crash that killed Princess Diana.

15

Cameras with telephoto lenses can take pictures from far away. Secretly aimed through windows or hedges, these cameras can make private life very public. Many complicated laws govern their use.

LIVE NEWS

Cameras, microphones, radios, satellites, and other devices, no matter how tiny, do not make news by themselves. They need media people. News crews must be standing by, able to rush to an event the moment it starts, so we can watch and listen "live as it happens."

TV reports are fast but fleeting. For in-depth information, people turn to print media.

THE POWER OF TV

In June 1994, a live news event showed the ever-increasing power of television. U.S. football and film star O. J. Simpson had been charged with killing his former wife, Nicole, and her friend Ronald Goldman. Then, Simpson disappeared. A friend contacted police to say that he and Simpson were on the freeway, driving across Los Angeles, and Simpson was threatening suicide.

After the chase, Simpson was arrested for murder. In October 1995, the world tuned in again for his televised trial. He was defended by attorney Johnnie Cochran, Jr. (below, center).

HOT PURSUIT

News crews raced to their helicopters. Spotting Simpson's white Ford Bronco weaving slowly through traffic, they flew above it. Onboard cameras sent TV pictures, via radio signals, to a local station that "patched" the pictures into the networks. Scheduled TV programs were interrupted as millions tuned in to view the drama of police chasing a famous suspect. It looked just like a TV show — but it was real life!

Around-the-clock news stations vied for viewers by trying to have more correspondents, in more cities, in more parts of the world, for local reporting wherever and whenever a story "broke."

ON-LINE NEWS

The Internet began to change the habits of news consumers. As computers went on-line, users could conveniently switch from their normal work on-screen to briefly check events on a news Web site. Employers argued that this kind of on-line usage was an abuse of the company's time and equipment. Employees argued that it was similar to listening to news headlines on an office radio.

www.imf.org

SO MANY SIGNALS

The technology for instant TV links was not new, but by the 1990s, broadband versions could pack enough coded signals into the available time to carry TV pictures that changed many times each second. By the year 2000, Cable News Network (CNN) was using over twenty satellites and reaching more than 150 million households in more than 200 countries.

Make news or take news? The Internet could do both.

By the late 1990s, information, including pictures and sounds from a pocket-size digital camera, could be sent from a laptop computer through a telecommunication system used by phones.

As major news events happened, TV and radio stations rushed their crews and equipment to the scenes. Trucks, cars, and even motorcycles acted as small mobile ground stations with dishes aligned to beam signals to satellites high in space.

STORED FOREVER

The 20th century began with recorded sound stored as a wavy groove in a gramophone disk. It ended with MP3, an all-electronic format for computers and the Internet. Other formats appeared in between and are still thriving.

DISC TECHNOLOGY

The 1980s brought compact discs (CDs), approximately seventy-five minutes of almost perfect sound stored as a digital code of microscopic pits on a shiny disc. The code is read by a laser beam that can be skipped to any part of the disc. In the 1990s, CD technology was reduced, yet extended, to include not only sounds but also pictures.

18

In the late 1990s, sales of DVD players soared, mainly for prerecorded movies or collections of TV shows. Home-use DVD players that could also record did not arrive until the 2000s.

MiniDiscs (MDs) were designed to be re-recordable, ultra-convenient, and anti-joggable inside personal players. MDs hold as much information as CDs but are only about a quarter of the size.

MP3 audio files can be played on, as well as manipulated by, a computer. They can also be fed into a memory "stick" for use in a home MP3 music system or in a tiny, personal MP3 player.

LESS, BUT MORE

The reduced version of the CD was the MD, or MiniDisc, announced by Sony in May 1991. It had the same sound content and quality as a CD but was only 2.5 inches (64 mm) across and could be used to record and re-record. The tiny, personal MD player soon became a must-have fashion item. The CD's extended version was the DVD, or Digital Versatile Disc. The same size as a CD, a DVD holds seven to eight times more information — enough for all the sounds and images of a full-length movie, plus outtakes, director's comments, and other extras.

MUSIC ON-LINE

The no-moving-parts, all-digital-electronic MP3 format was designed for sending sound along telecommunication lines, such as over the Internet, for storage on a computer disk. MP3 compresses the original files of recorded sounds, so a typical song takes only minutes, rather than hours, to send by Internet or e-mail.

Even in the 2000s, demand still exists for recordings on vinyl disks. Some audio enthusiasts prefer the slight inconsistencies and imperfections, saying that vinyl sounds warm and human, while CDs seem cold and impersonal.

COPYRIGHT ON TRIAL

For years, people have copied vinyl records and CDs. This practice did not interfere greatly with copyright laws, provided it was for personal use only. Putting music on the Internet, however, made it available to millions, often for free. The recorded music industry reacted by suing organizations, such as Napster, that made MP3 Internet files available. The controversy raged into the 2000s.

Napster representatives frequently faced the media.

VIRTUAL MOVIES

The year 1995 saw a landmark event in moviemaking — *Toy Story* — the world's first entirely computer-generated feature film. It had no real-life actors, no models, no hand-drawn animation. It was virtual.

The scaly, scary stars of Jurassic Park *were a combination of scale models, full-size robotics, hands-on animation, and computer graphics.*

Toy Story's stars, Woody, the old-timer, and space-age Buzz Lightyear, and their toy friends took as much as a million hours of computer processing time. Toy Story 2 *(1999) was also a huge hit.*

RESETTING THE STANDARD

Two years earlier, U.S. director Steven Spielberg had set new standards in special effects with his movie *Jurassic Park*, the story of dinosaurs re-created in the modern world. Some of the trickiest scenes featured interactions between the film's real-life actors and its modeled, computerized, or animated dinosaurs. The interplay between real and virtual was a problem *Toy Story* did not face.

BEYOND EFFECTS

Both films were smash hits, but not just for having groundbreaking special effects. They were both promoted with a blitz of advertising and a vast array of toys, games, theme meals, and other spin-off merchandise. Satisfied moviegoers thought they also had strong storylines, drama, sadness, humor, and happy endings — the classic ingredients of fine films. Other movie "firsts" have passed by more quietly because the films themselves were less memorable.

There are actually only a few soldier droids in *The Phantom Menace*. Computers adjusted the size and slightly twisted the same body shape for each droid. Each one was also randomly assigned a weapon and told its actions for the battle scene — again, all by computer.

BACK TO THE FUTURE

A final 1990s' blockbuster, *Star Wars Episode 1: The Phantom Menace* promised a lot. It was the first part of the cosmically successful space saga that began in 1977. The film had dazzling special effects, wall-to-wall advertising, and an endless variety of merchandise, yet it failed to capture the magic of the original.

CGI DINOSAURS

Computer-generated imagery (CGI) begins with a computer "map" of an object using points in three dimensions — height, width, and depth. The map may originally come from a life-size model. The points are linked in the computer by math equations, which allow them to move in relation to each other, but only within certain limits.

Lines join map points to give the impression of overall covering (skin).

Movement of leg also makes skin on flank "stretch."

21

Titanic (1997) captivated viewers with its special effects, which included a life-size mock-up of one side of the ship. For views of the other side, the film was flipped (turned left to right), and the crew wore hats with reversed "mirror" writing.

THE MEDIA ON THE MEDIA

In *The Truman Show* (1998), Jim Carrey plays Truman Burbank, who thinks he leads a normal life. In fact, however, Truman has existed, from birth, in a giant TV set. His family and friends are actors, and the rest of the world tunes in to watch — the ultimate "reality TV." The movie is a powerful comment on media manipulation.

IT COULD HAPPEN TO YOU!

Truman suspects that someone is watching him. Of course, everyone is.

ON FILM

In the 1990s, almost no mass-market feature movie made by an industrialized Western nation was spared from having computerized special effects. Besides the space and science-fiction blockbusters, however, the world saw many other cinema trends.

BOLLYWOOD?

The biggest center for making feature films in the 1990s was not Hollywood, in the United States, but Bollywood, in India. "Bollywood" is the nickname that was given to India's highly productive and successful film industry. Throughout the decade, it regularly produced eight to nine hundred movies, per year, in more than a dozen languages, including Hindi, Bengali, Gujarati, and Tamil. The biggest moneymaker of the decade was *Hum Aapke Hain Kaun* (1994), starring Bollywood's leading actor and actress, Shah Rukh Khan and Madhuri Dixit. Each of these stars could command half a million dollars or more per project.

HISTORY REPEATS ITSELF

Gripping drama adapted from history still scooped up the awards. For 1993, the Oscar for Best Picture went to *Schindler's List*, a harrowing tale of Nazi Germany. For 1995, it went to *Braveheart*, a portrayal of Scottish freedom fighter William Wallace.

One new trend was movies adapted from video and computer games. Characters and plots were already familiar from playing the games. Super Mario Brothers (1993), which involves reptile-fighting plumbers, was an early example.

Director Steven Spielberg had made not one but seven of the all-time greatest movies. Not until his 1993 movie Schindler's List, however, was his work first formally recognized — with not one but seven Oscars.

SCARY EARNINGS

By far, the film that made the most money compared to its cost was the apparently real horror tale *The Blair Witch Project* (1999). Estimates of its budget vary from $22,000 to $100,000 — about one day's food expenses for a big Hollywood movie. Yet, in just a year, *Blair Witch*'s box-office earnings were over $140 million. Its Internet, word-of-mouth, and specialty magazine promotions added to its spooky secrecy and "underground" appeal.

The Blair Witch Project *was directed by Daniel Myrick and Eduardo Sanchez.*

THRILLS AND CHILLS

Action thrillers, usually with equal portions of drama, humor, suspense, and horror, were huge hits. They included *Speed* (1994) and its sequels and *Scream* (1996) and its sequels. Of course, no decade since the 1960s was complete without superspy James Bond in the most profitable film series ever. Bond ended the millennium with *The World Is Not Enough* (1999).

In Scotland's 13th-century fight for independence, the rallying cry came from William Wallace. In the 20th century, it came from Australian star Mel Gibson, in the movie Braveheart.

Many Bollywood movies featured boy-meets-girl, boy-loses-girl, boy-triumphs-over-adversity-and-wins-girl traditional plots with happy endings — and often with songs.

Still strong in 2000, Britpoppers Mel Blatt (right) and Natalie Appleton, of the R&B and hip-hop influenced All Saints, accept the MTV Europe music video award for best pop group.

M USICAL DREAMS

Popular music largely played it safe during the 1990s. Dozens of already established styles continued, from heavy metal and progressive rock to gangsta rap, hip hop, and mass-market, sugarcoated pop. Still, two new trends also made headlines.

BRITPOP

From about 1994, music journalists were talking about "Britpop," referring to guitar-based bands that played lively, English-style songs with catchy tunes and without the "rock-god" strutting and screaming guitar solos of U.S.-based bands such as Aerosmith, Bon Jovi, and Van Halen.

Britpop group Blur was honored at the Brit Awards, a major music event, in 1995, and the number of awards grew steadily, with Grammys, MTVs, MOJOs, MOBOs, BBCs, Q Magazines, Billboards, and NMEs.

LEADERS OF THE PACK

Leading Britpop groups were Suede with the album *Suede* (1993), Blur with *Parklife* (1994), Pulp with *Different Class* (1995), and the argumentative, often drunk and violent, Oasis, with its phenomenally successful albums *Definitely Maybe* (1994) and *(What's the Story) Morning Glory?* (1995). In the fickle world of modern music, however, Britpop was no longer new by the late 1990s, and so, became less popular.

24

Prescott with wife, Pauline

THE RISKY BANDWAGON

Popular music's influence often drew public figures hoping to look "cool" by being seen with the latest stars. This ploy, however, could backfire. At the 1998 Brit Awards, a member of the very socialistic Liverpool band Chumbawamba poured water over British Labour Party politician John Prescott.

Through the 1990s, the media of television and popular music continued to feed off of each other. Dedicated music channel MTV led the way.

BOYZ AND GIRLZ

The second trend was boy or girl bands. Some could sing a little, dance in certain ways, and perhaps play instruments, but all were groomed for multimedia consumption by ever-younger audiences. British bands included Take That, Boyzone, Spice Girls, and All Saints. When Take That split up in 1996, special phone helplines were swamped by tearful girl fans. From the ashes of Take That rose a pop superstar of the late 1990s — Robbie Williams.

The Spice Girls burst onto the pop music scene in 1996 with Wannabe. *Only four years later, they were pursuing solo careers.*

After Princess Diana's death, Elton John's new version of "Candle in the Wind" became the biggest-selling record ever — over 30 million copies in 37 days.

MEDIA MEETS SPORTS

A major area of growth for the media involved their links with sports. Players and competitors alike joined the growing army of commentators, announcers, summarizers, and analyzers for TV, radio, books, and magazines.

The World Wrestling Federation (WWF) brought grappling back to the big time.

SPORTS ON THE SET

More than ever, sports events were organized around television coverage, especially under pressure from advertisers. International soccer matches held in Asia started very late at night to catch the sport's main market of early-evening viewers in Europe. In Britain, the commercial-free BBC lost several major sports, including Formula One auto racing and International Test-Match Cricket. Commercial channels such as ITV and Sky could afford to pay much larger amounts for the broadcasting rights.

In 1999, Michael Jordan retired as basketball's greatest — again. Basketball's "bad boy," Dennis Rodman, was famous for his infamous reputation.

The 1998 Soccer World Cup in France and the 2000 Olympic Games in Sydney, Australia, were the decade's most complex televised events. Even a standard league soccer match demanded a huge TV crew and dozens of cameras.

JORDAN
23

Many governments banned alcohol and tobacco sponsorships to keep impressionable young people from being exposed to the ads.

HELP OR HINDRANCE?

The increasing technology in media coverage, especially TV, led to problems in some sports. Slow-motion replays became so common that incidents were being shown several times within seconds, undermining the judgment and authority of referees and umpires. Some sports, especially football in America and rugby in Britain, turned replays to best advantage. Rugby referees, for example, are able to ask for the opinions of colleagues monitoring TV replays on multiple screens.

"It was out." "No, in." "Out!" "In!"

HOT MEDIA PROPERTIES

Sports stars were hot properties. Basketball greats Michael Jordan and Shaquille O'Neal, U.S. golf phenomenon Tiger Woods, German Formula One race ace Michael Schumacher, and Brazil's soccer wizard Renaldo got paid more in a month than many people earn in a lifetime.

MEDIA DREAM

Some stars earned even more outside their sports than within them, doing TV and radio interviews, putting their names on columns for newspapers and magazines, presenting videos, and, of course, showing advertisers' names and logos on their clothing and equipment. In 1999, the worlds of sports and pop music collided when England and Manchester United soccer star David Beckham married Victoria "Posh Spice" Adams of the Spice Girls. A royal wedding could hardly attract more attention. Posh 'n' Becks became the dream couple for media and advertising.

THE NEW MILLENNIUM

Looking back to 1900, the media included books; newspapers; posters; visual arts, such as painting, sculpture, and photography; and live performance. Sound recording and movies were in their infancy. Radio was experimental. Who could predict the future?

The Y2K bug hit cash machines in Japan.

MEDIA TAKEOVER

Even in 1950, there was little TV, no magnetic tapes or compact discs, and, of course, no personal computers or Internet. Just fifty years later, the media have changed beyond recognition, not only in their technology, such as thumb-size digital cameras and Internet-ready mobile phones, but also in their ever-increasing involvement in daily life.

Many millennium celebrations in the year 2000 were gigantic mediafests. At one of them, Australia's Sydney Harbour Bridge became the world's biggest fireworks holder.

ELECTRO-WARNING

Not only the media, but also business, industry, travel, and even education rely more and more on computerized electronic systems. Various Year 2000, or Y2K, computer "bugs" threatened global system disruption, but most failed to have an impact. If such bugs, however, affected the news media, people could not be warned about them or find out how to prepare for them.

MEDIA MANIPULATION

For many people, everyday conversation is no longer about local news, business, or even the weather. More likely, it is about the newest pop star's clothes, last night's TV shows, or the most recent movie on DVD. People, increasingly, are experiencing the world through the pictures and words of the media rather than in reality. Can we trust the media to present an honest, truthful version, or do they manipulate, for their own purposes, what we see, hear, and feel?

Internet videophones, palm-size computers, and ultrathin, foldaway screens are some of the new media products in development.

MEDIA FUTURE

The media hold unique positions of power and influence. They inform, entertain, and comfort us, but they also change our opinions and persuade us — maybe to depend on them even more than we do already. The last century saw amazing changes happen at ever-increasing speeds. One prediction seems certain — more changes, even faster, in the 21st century.

CURLING UP . . .

. . . with a good book is an age-old tradition. Multimedia can provide an electronic book with flexi-screen pages that turn just like paper ones. They show words and pictures from a pea-size memory chip. Pictures can be moving or animated, with sounds, too — to sing you to sleep.

A computer as convenient as a paperback book

With the spread of computers in the 1970s, some people thought that print media would fade and die, but more book titles are being published today than ever before.

Today's news gathering methods would baffle reporters of the 1900s. As then, headlines usually contain bad news, but "hard" news now is often replaced with showbiz gossip. Showbiz sells!

· TIME LINE ·

	WORLD EVENTS	HEADLINES	MEDIA EVENTS	TECHNOLOGY	THE ARTS
1990	•*Gulf War breaks out as Iraq invades Kuwait*	•*Nelson Mandela freed from jail in South Africa*	•*Mandela tribute concert at London's Wembley Stadium*	•*Laser videodisc introduced*	•*Johnny Depp stars in* Edward Scissorhands •*Crichton:* Jurassic Park
1991	•*Breakup of USSR* •*Yugoslavia: civil war* •*Gulf War ends*	•*Boris Yeltzin defeats communist candidate in Russia's first direct presidential election*	•*Nirvana starts grunge music* •*Whole encyclopedia put on pocket computer*	•*Philips introduces Compact Disc Interactive (CD-I) player*	•*Ridley Scott:* Thelma and Louise •*Jostein Gaarder:* Sophie's World
1992	•*U.S.: race riots in Los Angeles* •*Somalia devastated by civil war and famine*	•*World leaders meet at Rio de Janeiro Earth Summit to solve global pollution problems*	•*Michaelangelo virus infects computers worldwide*	•*Testing starts on digital AM radio broadcasts* •*Testing starts on videophones*	•*Brian Eno:* Nerve Net •*Jeff Koons:* Puppy
1993	•*U.S.: Clinton becomes president* •*Bosnia-Herzegovina: civil war*	•*Palestine Liberation Organization (PLO) and Israel sign peace agreement*	•*Schindler's List finally wins Oscar for Spielberg*	•*Intel introduces Pentium chip*	•*Andrew Lloyd Webber:* Sunset Boulevard •*Björk:* Debut •*Nyman:* The Piano
1994	•*South Africa: Mandela is first black president* •*Rwanda: civil war*	•*U.S. baseball strike cancels World Series for first time since 1904*	•*O. J. Simpson arrested for murder after slow-speed, televised police chase*	•*Digital satellite TV offered in U.S.* •*Computer Zip drive stores up to 100 MB*	•*Tom Hanks stars in* Forrest Gump •*Tarantino:* Pulp Fiction •*Weir:* Blond Eckbert
1995	•*U.S.: terrorist bomb blast in Oklahoma City* •*Tokyo: nerve gas attacks on subways*	•*Kobe, Japan, destroyed by earthquake* •*Israeli leader Yitzak Rabin assassinated*	•*O. J. Simpson verdict:* "not guilty" •*Toy Story is first totally digital feature film*	•*WebTV combines Internet and television* •*Sony demonstrates flat TV screen*	•*The Prodigy:* Music for the Jilted Generation •*Ron Howard:* Apollo 13
1996	•*"Mad cow" disease; bans on British beef* •*Afghanistan: Taliban Muslims seize power*	•*Britain's Prince Charles and Princess Diana divorce after 3-year separation*	•*FCC approves a standard for digital high-definition television (HDTV)*	•*Bayliss wind-up radio receivers* •*Nikon E2 digital camera*	•*Spice Girls:* Spice •*Madonna stars in* Evita
1997	•*UK returns Hong Kong to China* •*UK: Blair named prime minister*	•*Princess Diana and Dodi Fayed die in Paris car crash* •*Mother Teresa dies*	• *IBM computer defeats chess champ Garry Kasparov*	•*Kodak point-and-shoot digital camera* •*DVDs introduced*	•*J. K. Rowling:* Harry Potter and the Philospher's Stone (Sorcerer's Stone)
1998	•*Birth of the euro currency* •*South Africa: Truth and Reconciliation Report*	•*U.S. House of Representatives votes to impeach President Clinton*	•*U.S. Justice Department sues Microsoft "monopoly"*	•*Apple iMac* •*MP3s* •*Pentium II processor*	•*Jim Carrey stars in* The Truman Show •*Peter Davies:* The Hot One Hundred
1999	•*Serbs drive Albanians out of Kosovo* •*India and Pakistan: nuclear testing crisis*	•*Clinton acquitted in impeachment trial* •*NATO launches air strikes on Yugoslavia*	•*Melissa is worst computer virus to date* •*World worries about Y2K computer bugs*	•*New home video games have 128-bit operating systems*	•*Lucas:* The Phantom Menace •*Santana:* Supernatural •*Philip Glass:* Dracula

GLOSSARY

analog: related to a form of electronic transmission, as in conventional radios and telephones, that adds signals of varying frequency or amplitude (height) to waves of alternating electromagnetic current.

apartheid: a policy of racial segregation in South Africa that discriminated both politically and economically against non-European citizens.

binary: related to a system of numbers that has a base of two (0 and 1) rather than the usual base of ten (0 through 9).

broadband: related to a communication network with a frequency range that is divided into many separate channels, all transmitting signals at the same time.

chips: small, wafer-thin slices of a semiconductor material, such as silicon, that are used in making integrated circuitry for digital electronic systems.

digital: related to an electronic system that uses numbers, or digits, usually 0 and 1, to form codes that represent information, or data.

infrastructures: the basic frameworks and installations, including buildings and equipment, required to carry out the activities of systems or organizations.

paparazzi: photographers who relentlessly follow celebrities, trying to take candid photographs to sell to the highest bidder, usually for publication in print or broadcast media.

patched: connected by means of electronic circuits and devices.

reality TV: television programming that records the activities of people supposedly acting naturally, without interference from cameras, interviewers, or directors, sometimes as part of a contest or game to win large sums of money or valuable prizes.

MORE BOOKS TO READ

1900–2000: The Electronic Age. 20th Century Science and Technology (series). Steve Parker (Gareth Stevens)

Cyber Space: Virtual Reality and the World Wide Web. Megatech (series). David Jefferis (Crabtree)

Digital Revolution. 20th Century Inventions (series). Stephen Hoare (Raintree Steck-Vaughn)

The End of Apartheid: A New South Africa. Point of Impact (series). Richard L. Tames (Heinemann)

How the Future Began: Communications. Anthony Wilson (Kingfisher)

Make Your Own Web Page! A Guide for Kids. Ted Pedersen and Francis Moss (Econo-Clad Books)

Marc Andreessen: Web Warrior. Techies (series). Daniel Ehrenhaft (Twenty-First Century Books)

Multimedia Magic. Robert L. Perry (Franklin Watts)

Shawn Fanning: Napster and the Music Revolution. Techies (series). Christopher Mitten (Twenty-First Century Books)

Techno Lab: How Science Is Changing Entertainment. Carol Anderson and Robert Sheely (Silver Moon Press)

WEB SITES

The Animated Internet.
www.learnthenet.com/english/animate/animate.htm

How Stuff Works: Consumer Electronics.
www.howstuffworks.com/category.htm?cat=Consum

How We Make a Movie: Pixar's Animation Process.
www.pixar.com/howwedoit

The Mandela Page.
www.anc.org.za/people/mandela

Due to the dynamic nature of the Internet, some web sites stay current longer than others. To find additional web sites, use a reliable search engine with one or more of the following keywords: *apartheid, Bollywood, Britpop, CDs, computer history, cyber cafés, digital electronics, DVDs, Internet, mobile phones, Princess Diana,* and *Y2K.*

INDEX

32